D1321164

Evening Standard

IMAGES OF LONDON

Evening Standard

IMAGES OF LONDON

Compiled by Jennifer Seed
and Carol D'Praser

Words by Angus McGill

Breedon Books
Publishing Company
Derby

First published in Great Britain by
The Breedon Books Publishing Company Limited
44 Friar Gate, Derby, DE1 1DA.
1995

ISBN 1 85983 001 3

Printed and bound by Butler & Tanner, Frome, Somerset.

Cover separations and design by Evening Standard, London.

Cover printed by Premier Print, Nottingham.

Acknowledgements

Evening Standard Production Team

Cover design by Jennifer Seed

We would like to thank the following people for their invaluable contributions towards this book:

David Sheppard, Brian Jackson and the staff of Associated Newspapers Picture Library for photographic help, resources and patience.

Staff photographers past, and Dennis Jones and Ken Towner present.

Simon Murray, Ian Roberts and Nick Cave for help with producing the artwork for the jacket.

Clare Emery for reading the copy.

A special thanks to Tower Bridge for the historic photograph of the bridge under construction on page 28 and Pavilion Books Limited for the photograph on page 23.

Lizbeth Gayle and Sarah Brown from the RCHM Library.

The National Monuments Record for historic early photographs of London. The NMR provides open access to 75,000 photographs and 12,000 measured drawings of London buildings and an extensive reference library. Archive material can be consulted on request.

The NMR in London
55 Blandford Street,
London, W1H 3AF.
Tel 0171 208 8208
Fax 0171 224 5333

Public search rooms open:
Monday to Wednesday 10am – 5.30pm
Thursday 10am – 7pm
Friday 10am – 5pm

NATIONAL MONUMENTS RECORD

Contents

Great cities change almost as you look and not just the cities. The people who live in them change too. They stare at us incuriously from these pages, a moment in their lives captured and held. We stare back. It is the way they dress that strikes you first, then the body language, the life behind the eyes. Who are they? What are they up to? What happened next?

The newspaper photographers and others who made these pictures open window after window on a city we still share but sometimes hardly recognise. Was this how London and Londoners used to be? It is unsettlingly familiar but another country, another world.

Many of the buildings, at least, remain. Here is Georgian London, Victorian London, Edwardian London, here the often frenetic London of the twenties and thirties. Now London is cruelly at war, now newly at peace and on we go into the fifties and sixties, the London of the day before yesterday. This too belongs to history, the flower children and the beautiful people, the mods and rockers, the bouffant hairdos and Ford Cortinas.

As the years pass and the pages turn we see London booming, suffering, swinging, rioting, London in extremis and London in love. The rich and famous play their part, great buildings are never far away. At the heart of it, though, this is how things were for ordinary people in ordinary times. Extraordinary.

A Roof Over Our Heads

When London was Londinium and the Romans called the shots well-to-do Londoners lived in some style. Villas with all mod cons, central heating, slaves to run the bath. Their successors, toff and pleb, lived in a variety of dwellings. Here are some of them.

Across Trafalgar Square, through Admiralty Arch and straight along the Mall and you are at Buckingham Palace. You can't miss it. This was the view in 1924.

The garden front of Buckingham Palace, the other side which few see, snapped in 1889.

Apsley House before the World War One. The imposing Robert Adam mansion at Hyde Park Corner, then known as No 1 London, was presented to the Duke of Wellington by a grateful nation after Waterloo.

©RCHME/Crown Copyright

Nos 10, 11 and 12 Downing Street in 1887, a modest little street, jerrybuilt they say. Lord Salisbury was in No 10 at this time.

Number 10's famous front door seems in better form today.

Victorian children playing in the street in Deptford.

George Romney, the fashionable portrait painter, moved to this pleasant brick and clapboard Hampstead house in 1799. Hampstead was considered pretty smart even then.

1900: the Black Boy and a row of handsome wooden houses and shops in Mile End Road. The pub dated from the Armada, the houses and shops were not much younger. All came down to make way for Stepney Green Station in 1902.

Before Chelsea Bridge was rebuilt in 1934 there were four pillar dwellings, one on each corner. Mrs May, in the doorway, lived in this one for 30 years.

Hampstead grandees lived in fine Georgian houses like this one in Heath Street. They still do.
Peter O'Toole lived here when this picture was taken in 1971.

1934: swings and roundabouts newly installed in the yard of St George's Flats, St Pancras, attract a press photographer. 'London Children's Latest Playground,' reports his paper.

1934: new luxury flats in Sloane Avenue with electricity, lifts and central heating. The rents ranged from £90 to £170 a year. It was the first block of flats in London to be made completely of concrete.

1935: 'the latest semi-detached sun-trap houses now being created near Hampton Court are equipped with sun-bathing roofs and special large windows. The chimney pots are practically hidden.'

February 1944: Lord Woolton, Minister of Reconstruction, opens an exhibition of labour saving devices for the post-war kitchen. Among them is this new device. It produces water hot enough to make the tea.

February 1945: with the war over, news for some bombed-out Lambeth families. They can move from air raid shelters to this circle of 14 hutments made from curved asbestos.

April 1945: a sensation in Clerkenwell, a colony of the latest American prefabs.

Harold Wilson's house in Hampstead Garden Suburb. He bought it in 1947 when he was President of the Board of Trade, sold it 22 years later when he was Prime Minister. Estate agents valued it at £16,000.

February 1962: Southwark prefabs get new neighbours – six 18-storey tower blocks, hailed by the LCC as the tallest blocks of flats in London.

October 1976: 'Shadow Prices Minister Sally Oppenheim's home in Bishop's Avenue, Hampstead, which has been sold to Sheikh Ali Sindi of Saudi Arabia for £600.000.'

The River

The Thames is at the heart of it all. For 2,000 years Londoners have lived by it, worked on it, feared it and loved it.

Lean on London Bridge and look up river in 1910 and this is what you saw – the Pool of London alive with boats of all sort, cargo boats, pleasure boats, river boats, colliers, barges, tugs and skiffs, a vista of funnels, masts and sails, the banks lined with jetties, quays, docks and warehouses, one of the great working and trading rivers in the world.

August 1945: the Thames sailing barge *William Everard* arriving in the Pool of London with a cargo of 300 tons of palm kernels.

A Thames barge with its red sails passing Broadway Dock at Limehouse.

The waterfront that Dickens knew, ramshackle and noisome, labouring to keep ships victualled and afloat and sailors cheaply lodged.

The wooden Battersea Bridge, built in 1771 and immortalised by Whistler. It was replaced by the cast-iron bridge we know today in the 1880s.

Way upstream and a glimpse of an idyll, a life of seamless leisure celebrated in this sunlit afternoon at the Henley Regatta in the golden summer of 1911, caught by the extraordinary camera of Horace W.Nicholls.

High drama and low comedy at the 1912 Boat Race. Both boats sink.

Total decorum at the 1912 Henley Regatta. King George V and Queen Mary keep an eye on things from the Royal barge.

1930: unloading Soviet sweets and biscuits from the Russian steamer *Jan Rudzutak* at Hayes Wharf, London Bridge, to be sold by a cut price chain of stores.

1934: 'despite the recent heavy rainfalls the Thames is still at a very low level ...' as the caption says. Bad news this for the old Chelsea Bridge, hoping for a reprieve but soon to be replaced. The piles for the new bridge darkly gather.

March 1939: bargee skipper A.F.Lea, more than 60 years on the river man and boy.

July 1941: barges loaded with coal slip quietly along the Regent's Canal.

August 1944: the sun dances on the water as a pleasure steamer crammed with holiday-makers leaves Richmond and heads blithely down river.

In At The Birth

Some buildings seem to have been here for ever. But even the bigges

28   1890: everyone knows Tower Bridge. Here it is about halfway up. The Prince of Wales laid the foundation stone in 1881 and came back to open it with a tremendous do in 1894.

randest, most famous were also just so high not so long ago.

1907: Rotherhithe Tunnel, three years a'building, one more year to go, a remarkable feat of engineering. It is 4,860ft long and 48ft below high water mark to give big ships room to pass.

1903: stage 1 of the Savoy Hotel had been finished and open for four years. Now stage 2 had begun. The hotel was already a byword for luxury and expense. A double room with bath cost 60p a day.

1872: the Albert Memorial is almost finished. Queen Victoria is expected to visit soon. Then the scaffolding will come down. It will be a very great sensation.

1930: the Whitehall Theatre is almost finished. It is so clean and simple, writes the *Architect's Journal* in 1931, it makes the nearby Government offices look as if they need a shave. Ahead lie 24 years of Whitehall farces.

1937: the stately Alhambra that occupied this prime site in Leicester Square for many years did not take long to come down. Now the modernist new Odeon is going up at a rate of knots.

©RCHME/Crown Copyright

1978: the foundation stone of the National Westminster Tower was laid seven years ago. The builders have just to finish off the top bit and to get the last crane down from the roof and the bank can take possession of the tallest structure in Britain.

The Parks

No other great city has such a wealth of open spaces, rus in urbe an
so many acres of heath and common. Seen from the air London is a

This is Hampstead Heath. The *Evening Standard* has called it our greatest natural asset – 790 acres of park and
woodland, 26 ponds, rare bog life, swamps, sand slopes, the remnant of a medieval forest and an early
seventeenth-century manor house with marvellous art treasures. No other capital city can match it.

pen to us all. Such patrician gardens, so much fine parkland,
stonishingly green and pleasant land.

And this is Hampstead Heath again, London's irreplaceable expanse of open countryside, never the same two days running.

Whitehall seen across the lake of St James's Park, takes your breath away. This is one of the most spectacular skylines in Europe.

St James's Park, our most formal, most elegant park, with its lake and its waterbirds and, always in the background, the tangible presence of Buckingham Palace.

The ballet of the waterbirds with a trio of fountains against a backcloth of weeping willow. It is St James's Park again. Who could tire of it?

The St James's Park lake freezes all too rarely but when it does skaters come from miles around. This is how it looked in February 1954.

In 1905 the Barton-Rawdon airship made a trial flight and was the sensation of the hour. Thousands gathered in the grounds of Alexandra Palace where it was tethered to watch it rise majestically from its mooring and sail over London.

1902: it is Sunday in Rotten Row and everyone's dressed to kill.

June 1912: boating time on the Serpentine.

August 1922: children on holiday flock to the paddling pool in Bishop's Park, Fulham.

A remarkable pastoral scene in the heart of teeming London. In April 1926 Londoners awake to find several hundred Aberdeen sheep grazing in Hyde Park, peacefully attended by a shepherd and his dog.

July 1928: a heatwave in London and in Kensington Gardens the smart money is on tea in the shade.

March 1933:
young riders
pose with
their pony on
the railings in
Rotten Row.

October 1933 : a
brilliantly sunny
morning,
everyone's back
in town and the
place to see and
be seen is Hyde
Park. 'Little
Season in the
Park,' announced
the columnists.

July 1935: the cranes and gantries of London Docks crowd the skyline but, for children in Shadwell, the Memorial Park is the Riviera. An East End Lido we say.

May 1940: Battersea Park gets a new luxury cafe with a modernistic verandah and a lovely view of lawns, a waterfall and a lake.

London Zoo, April 1920: apparently a popular camel. Look at the crowd.

Whitsun 1950: elephants are always a star turn. This one, giving six children a ride, stops for a snack.

August 1953: a hot day and a cool sluice down for Lakshmi. London Zoo's 15-month-old elephant, a big draw in Children's Corner.

Easter Monday 1954: penguins are natural comedians. Here they are doing their Pall Mall clubmen sketch.

July 1959: the Children's Zoo re-opens in Regent's Park. The baby chimps, of course, are top of the bill.

July 1969: fans swing into into Hyde Park for the first appearance of the Rolling Stones for more than a year. The official estimate of the crowd is 200,000.

May 1965: the first occupants move into Lord Snowdon's revolutionary new aviary in Regent's Park. They include 30 whistling duck, spoon bills, crown cranes, plovers, kittiwakes and a keeper.

The Royals

Now adding presence to otherwise mundane daily events, now centre stage on occasions of spectacular ceremonial, the royal family is part of the everyday life of this great city.

The Coronation ceremony is over and the newly crowned young Queen and her consort return to the palace. As the magnificent gold state coach of George III passes the Victoria Memorial a mighty cheer goes up from the vast crowd. The Queen smiles and waves, the Duke smiles. A new reign, a new era, has begun.

Queen Victoria at 80, a small, sombre but arresting figure in the back of an open landau, bidding farewell to troops on their way to the Boer War.

The Canada Arch in Whitehall, part of the lavish decorations for the Coronation of King Edward VII. The Cenotaph occupies the site now.

We have here a very happy monarch. It is 1909 and King Edward VII's horse Minoru had just won the Derby.

King George V never managed a Derby winner but he too loved a day at the races. Here he is in the Royal box at Epsom in 1934.

George V laid many a foundation stone. In 1913 it was one for Australia House in the Strand but first there was the guard of honour to inspect.

A guard of honour for Queen Mary at Clapton in 1921. Then there was a new Nurse's Block to be opened.

In 1921 the new Southwark Bridge was finished. The King declared it well and truly open and drove across it with the Queen.

In 1928 Blackburn Rovers and Huddersfield Town came to Wembley for the FA Cup Final. Blackburn won and George V was there to present Harry Healless with the cup.

In 1929 it was the Prince of Wales's turn for Wembley. Bolton Wanderers won the FA Cup and the Prince shook hands with everyone.

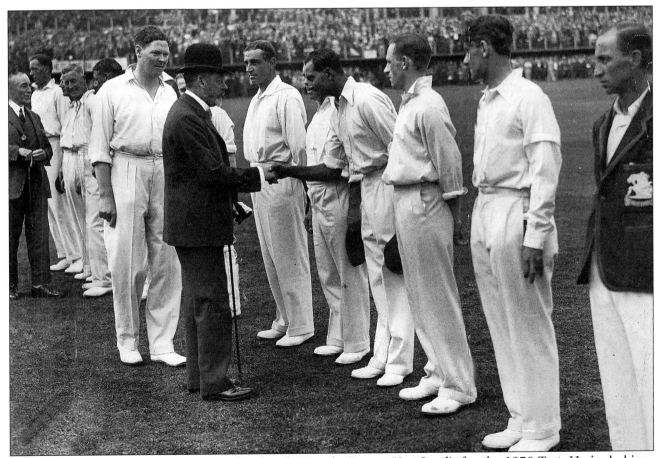

Day after day monarchs shake hand after hand. Here is George V at Lord's for the 1930 Test. He is shaking hands with K.S.Duleepsinhji.

The Duchess of York preferred tennis. So for her it was the 1931 Lawn Tennis Exhibition in Lady Crosfield's garden in Highgate and a chat with Helen Jacobs and Betty Nuthall.

When it comes to guards of honour you can't start too early. Princess Elizabeth, aged five, returns the salute at the 1931 Royal Tournament.

The big new Mount Pleasant sorting office got a stylish opening from the Duke and Duchess of York in 1934. They stayed on to do a bit of sorting themselves.

In 1934 the Duchess of York was off to the Dorchester for a charity tea to raise money for working girls. From one little girl she got a big bouquet, a bigger smile and a successful curtsey.

It is January 1936. King George V has died at Sandringham. Now his eldest son, King Edward VIII, and his brother, the Duke of York, follow their father's coffin to Westminster Hall for the Lying in State.

June 1936: and the new King and his brothers, the Dukes of York, Gloucester and Kent, ride out of Buckingham Palace.

May 1936, and, with ancient ceremony, the approaching coronation is proclaimed at St James's Palace, Charing Cross, Temple Bar and, above, at the Royal Exchange.

July 1936, confident and popular, the new King presents new colours to the Grenadier, Coldstream and Scots Guards in Hyde Park. There was no hint of the violent event immediately ahead.

A drama on Constitution Hill.
A would-be assassin is
pounced on and frogmarched
away. Just off camera King
Edward VIII rides by and on
the roadway under the horses'
hooves lies the man's loaded
revolver.

The man who tried to shoot
the king. The story and the
picture went round the
world.

By December the brief reign of Edward VIII was over. Outside the Houses of Parliament a shocked crowd reads the news. The King has abdicated.

November 1946: King George VI, Queen Elizabeth and the two Princesses arrive at the London Palladium for the Royal Variety Performance.

April 26, 1948: under the dome of St Paul's Cathedral the King and Queen give thanks for their Silver Wedding Day.

May 1953: Princess Elizabeth will be crowned Queen Elizabeth II next week and school children all over London become proud owners of Coronation mugs and little Union Jacks on sticks.

The Queen's glittering gold coach drawn by eight Windsor greys, passes the huge crowds in Trafalgar Square on its way round the processional route from the Abbey.

Coronation Day. The Queen, wearing the sovereign's Crown of State and flanked by the Archbishops of
Canterbury and York, starts her slow progress out of Westminster Abbey.

For some the climax of Coronation Day. The Queen and her family line the balcony of Buckingham Palace as the vast crowd below waves, cheers, roars.

Getting There . . .

Getting there and getting back has ever been a major problem in these parts. Londoners have tried everything, horses, carts, carriages, sedan chairs, trams, buses, bikes, underground trains, skateboards, helicopters, hansom cabs, taxis. Some have tried out the new-fangled motor car. Others have walked.

In the battle between the horse bus and the motor bus it is plain which is winning. Look at Cheapside, jammed with the new, reliable, rubber-tyred, open-topped double-decker motor buses. King Edward himself, they say, drives a motor car.

Knightsbridge in 1888 and they are building the Hyde Park Hotel on the left. When it opens there will be lots of work for all those hansom cabs.

The four-wheeled cab is smarter of course. But will the horse reach the corner?

You think the traffic jam is a recent invention? Look at London Bridge in 1867.

Ludgate Circus in 1890. A spanking new steam train crosses the bridge but horses still pull the bus underneath it.

The Strand in 1895. Mark my words the horse bus is here to stay.

In the year 1900 the London General Omnibus Ltd ran 1,348 buses like this one. It employed 16,790 horses, covered 31 million miles in the year and carried 199,575,529 passengers.

Post early for Christmas. The Christmas rush at Mount Pleasant in 1908.

1912, the junction of Oxford Street and Tottenham Court Road and total victory for the motor bus. London is criss-crossed with routes and Open Air to Everywhere is the slogan on the new bus maps.

1912: a useful new service – the No 38. Victoria Station to Epping Forest.

The Strand in 1919. Five buses, all packed. A taxi. A van. Not a horse in sight.

The new woman of 1910 put on her boater and got on her bike . . .

. . . after first having had
some lessons at the City
Bicycle School next door
to the Turk's Head in
Chequer Street.

For the new woman of 1919 the new omnibuses present familiar problems and well understood solutions: elbows. shoulders, the tactics of the sales.

1936: new streamline single-decker buses are introduced. "They are the LAST WORD IN COMFORT. Lucky Londoners !" read the caption to this picture.

1890: the Prince of Wales goes to Stockwell in a horse-drawn carriage to open the world's first electric tube railway. It goes from Stockwell to King William Street. Stockwell flies every flag it can find.

1919: the Metropolitan Line introduces new carriages. They do away with strap-hanging by doing away with the straps.

1928: London's newest, biggest, most advanced underground station opens: Piccadilly Circus. It has the latest of everything including this battery of automatic ticket-issuing machines.

1 October 1968: St Pancras Station is 100 years old today. Sir George Gilbert Scott designed it, using his rejected plans for government offices in Whitehall.

April 1946: family and friends gather at Liverpool Street Station to wave goodbye to a train-load of Empire Brides, off to join their husbands in Australia. First stop Tilbury, then the boat.

1904: one of the Great Western Railway's spanking new County Class locomotives starts its working life, serving the West Country from Brunel's elegant Paddington Station.

A railway terminus can usually reckon on a ripe old age. Fenchurch Street Stations don't make old bones though. There have been three. This was the second, photographed in 1912. It was rebuilt in 1935 and is still a terminus. Rather a minor one now.

This little freight train from Hornsey sent a line of steam over Holborn Viaduct every day as it left Snow Hill tunnel.

1965 saw a strike of porters at St Pancras Station. Passengers cheerfully managed.

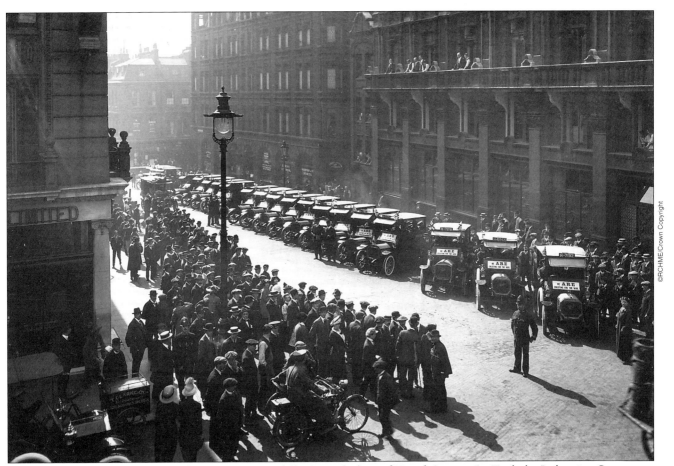

August 1914: the AA parades its new Automobile Association of Road Scouts In Taxis in Leicester Square. The idea is that if a member breaks down an AA man will arrive in a taxi.

1926: the Embankment during the General Strike. The cars stopped. The drivers walked.

1983: Hell's Angels don't walk. They pick up their women and roar off on their bikes.

The Markets

A great city takes some feeding. That is the job of the markets. They have other roles too. In no other city are they so many and so various.

July 1937: Jim Sainsbury, the Covent Garden basket-carrying champion, gets up to 22 baskets – 20 on his head and one in each hand.

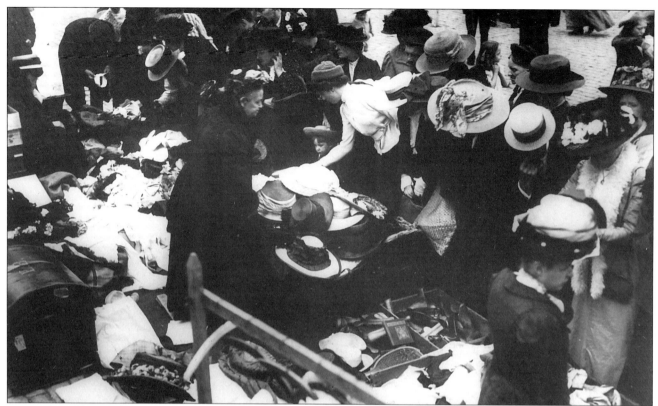

1910: the old Caledonian Market just north of King's Cross, known at that time as the Rag Fair and famous for the vast variety of its junk. Amazing bargains were rumoured. It has now moved to Bermondsey.

December 1931: enormous crowds fill Petticoat Lane, the famous East End street market, for early Christmas shopping.

1910: Smithfield, London's handsome meat market, horse-drawn waggons waiting and buyers in boaters.

©RCHME/Crown Copyright

©RCHME/Crown Copyright

1924: Armour and Co's stand in Smithfield, the company name picked out in sausages on the sides of pork.

November 1958: members of the Stock Exchange hear today's dramatic news from the Government Broker. The bank rate is going down half a per cent.

9 September 1949: the pound is devalued. The Stock Exchange is closed. Tic-tac men pass the latest news from one end of Throgmorton Street to the other.

16 October 1964: overnight election results indicate a Labour government and heavy dealing is certain. Brokers and jobbers press round the doors of the Stock Exchange. They open at 9.30am.

The Blitz

From September 1940 to May 1941 London was bombed every single night killed and 350,000 houses damaged or destroyed. Three years later, just a V2s, first the flying bombs, then the even more deadly rockets. Half a centu

Some say this is the war's most moving picture. At the height of the blitzkrieg, with London blazing on every side, St Paul's Cathedral stands serene and unharmed.

metimes there were daylight raids as well. More than 15,000 people were
war seemed almost over at last, London faced a new ordeal, the V1s and
ter and we can still see the scars.

Warehouses blaze along the Thames.

Fire bombs ravage
Hatton Gardens.

Not many windows left in Regent Street.

Oxford Street gets it. John Lewis is gutted.

Rescuing the mannequins.

A salvage sale in Oxford Street. Everything Must Go.

The morning after in Stationers' Hall. Sir William Domville hangs askew.

East Enders rescue what they can.

Some clearing up to do in Fetter Lane.

All that remained of the great library of Holland House. The historic Jacobean mansion in Kensington was destroyed in a raid in October 1940. The beautiful old house blazed for hours. Who are these men in hats so interested in the books?

Business as usual in Theobalds Road.

Rubble all round the Tower of London.

Some changes to the view from St Paul's.

The Palace of Westminster is an early casualty. One bomb badly damages the south wall of St Stephen's Porch and the tracery of its great window and bends Richard Coeur-de-Lion's sword.

Greenwich Observatory loses a dome. The thermometer on the left seems all right.

The Houses of Parliament were hit more than a dozen times. This is Cloister Court after a December raid in 1940. On 10 May 1941 the House of Commons was completely destroyed.

Jo-Jo, a Bayswater duck, gets an identification disc.

A Harrow schoolboy adds to his shrapnel collection.

The house is gone but Fluff's okay. His picture made the *New York Times*.

They have come to work. But where is the office?

Chest-high in the rubble of the Royal College of Surgeons, the bronze bust of William Owen, its Victorian conservator.

The air-raid shelter is Holland Park underground station. The tea comes from a watering can.

Sniffing for
escaping gas.

Bananas on the fruit stall! Someone's lucky day.

No windows or doors but the corner shop's still open.

Some minor repairs and no milk for the house next door.

A night shift for the girls of the Auxiliary Fire Service.

The altar has gone at St Stephen's, Southwark, but morning service is held as usual.

A bit of a draught but the phone's still working.

Fashion

The fair and the fashionable have always flocked to London. Whatever the mode of the moment, codpiece or crinoline, bustle, beauty spot or ring through the nose, London has led the way.

1966: 'mini-skirted girls protest outside the Christian Dior fashion house in London's Conduit Street today as the Dior Autumn and Winter Collection is shown within. The girls are members of the Society for the Preservation of Mini-Skirts.'

Left: 1918 : 'the Standard Suit. A photograph taken yesterday in a large City clothing establishment of the standard suit now being placed on the market. This suit, of the same material and colour as a length recently purchased by the King, costs £2 17s 6d.'

Right: 1917: 'misfits for Discharged Soldiers. Dissatisfaction is felt with the cheap reach-me-down suits served out to our discharged soldiers. It is stated that there are only three sizes and misfits are the rule. Mufflers are supplied in lieu of collars and ties. A specimen get-up.'

1921: 'a huge crowd, representative of all classes, attended the wedding at St Margaret's, Westminster, of Mr Edward Raylton Joicey MC and Miss Violet Loraine, the popular actress.'

1925: 'Mr Norman Hartnell, the ex-Cambridge undergraduate, with a striking brown Chantilly lace dress over flesh pink, entirely lined with lace and collared with ostrich feathers. One of his latest creations for Ascot.'

1934: 'Mrs Charles Sweeny leaving home to be presented at the third Court of the season last night. As Miss Margaret Whigham she was one of the most popular debutantes of 1931. Her gown is of pale coral pink crepe beauté.'

1933: 'the Prince of Wales continuing an example he set last year by wearing a "boater" at an aerial display on Saturday.'

1966: 'the Magnificent Seven of Carnaby Street. They run the principal shops in London's street of fashion.'

1967: 'LONDON: The windows are full of the latest 'in' clothes. Everything from the most mini of mini-dresses to the latest in men's jackets and trouser wear can be seen at the centre of the young man's fashion HQ, Carnaby Street.'

1967: 'top fashion model Twiggy with her Ford Mustang car.'

1967: 'Jean Shrimpton, Face of the 'Sixties.'

1968: 'rocker at Heathrow to meet Bill Haley and The Comets'

1970: 'fashion designer Mary Quant in an Oxford Street store signing autographs at the counter selling tights.'

1971: 'Carol Catkin and
Sharon Carpenter
wearing see-through
blouses in Regent Street.'

1974: 'Mick Jagger and his wife Bianca arriving at the Savoy for the charity fashion show tonight.'

1985: 'punks marching for CND.'

Taking to the Streets

As a rule Londoners keep their cool. Differences of view are
seriously pursued without bloody noses. Except sometimes.

'Anti-German Crisis. Riotous Scenes in the East End. Rioters Throwing Furniture Out Of A Window in
High Street, Poplar.' Published in 1919.

Striking dockers in the Pool of London in 1886.

Hyde Park, 1913: the London Contingent of the Women's Suffrage Pilgrimage march to the great demonstration with banners flying.

Miss Elsa Myers
addresses a
suffragette meeting at
West Ham.

The 1913 Derby: suffragette Emily Davidson throws herself beneath the hooves of the King's horse.

June 1913: suffragettes in white dresses and black sashes at the funeral of Emily Davidson.

2 August 1919: and the police are on strike. They barrack a fellow policeman still on duty as they march through Kennington.

5 August 1919 and there's looting in the London Road. 'Boot shops suffered severely,' read the caption.

28 September 1919 and the railways go on strike. Office workers, waiting on Blackfriars Bridge, get a lift home by horse and cart.

30 September 1919 and still no trains. Government lorries deliver the fish to Billingsgate.

1920 and the Lyons teashops strike, an unheard of event. It began when Mrs Sparkes was sacked. Now she leads the teashop girls on a protest march to Tower Hill.

March 1924 and the buses and trams have struck. Friends and neighbours charter their own lorries.

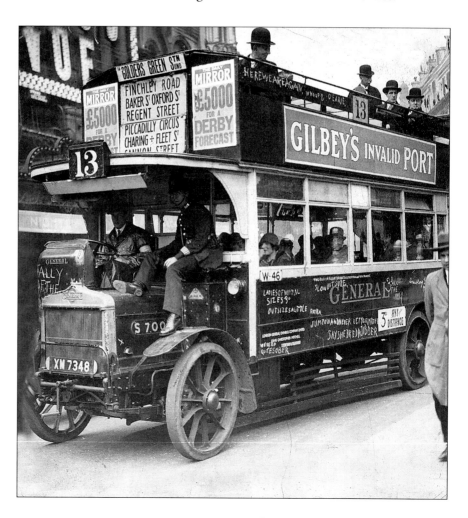

A volunteer drives the bus and a policeman rides shotgun. It is May 1926 and the General Strike has just begun.

The General Strike settles in. Lorries delivering food travel in convoy past Mappin and Webb in the city, each with two armed soldiers in the back.

Off to work in the General Strike. He is something in the city and he has breakfast as he roller skates in.

The General Strike gets bitter, sometimes violent. Lorries travelling in convoy through London are now protected by an armoured car and a truckload of steel-helmeted troops.

November 1932 and violent clashes between unemployed demonstrators and mounted police in the streets around Hyde Park.

February 1933 and Mr Emrhys Llewellyn, secretary of the National Unemployed Workers Association addresses a mass meeting on Tower Hill. He had been released from Brixton Prison the night before.

December 1933: British fascists form a riot squad, a gang of young men with an armoured car, to speed to trouble spots at a moment's notice.

March 1934 and mounted police try to disperse hunger marchers in Trafalgar Square.

February 1936 and there's a meat strike. Smithfield Market, usually teeming, is all but deserted.

October 1936 and British fascists march along the Embankment.

December 1936: the abdication of
Edward Vlll is imminent. Women
demonstrate in Downing Street.

May 1937: the buses are on strike again and Oxford Circus tube is under seige.

November 1966: students sing protest songs outside the door of the London School of Economics' disciplinary committee.

March 1964: ban-the-bomb
demonstrators march 20-abreast
down Whitehall.

September 1966: anti-Vietnam War
demonstrators making for the Labour Party HQ
in Smith Square.

September 1966: opposing views are expressed outside Marlborough House before the Commonwealth Prime Ministers Conference.

January 1967: fights break out in Trafalgar Square and Whitehall during the Support Ian Smith rally.

June 1967: two anti-Vietnam demonstrators on the course at Ascot immediately ahead of the Royal procession.

August 1967: Biafran students protest in Downing Street.

February 1975: Bunny Girls demonstrate outside the Playboy Club in Park Lane. Some of the girls wanted a union. Some didn't.

Sport

Great sporting events have always been part of London life – the cup ties and Test Matches, the Boat Race, the dramas of the ring and the Centre Court and the darts match at the pub.

Wembley 1966 and national pride sweeps the country. England wins the World Cup and, as jubilant supporters sweep on to the pitch and players hug and cry, Bobby Moore rides high on the shoulders of his team mates, showing the precious trophy to the world.

April 1923 and the first FA Cup Final at Wembley. A cameraman snaps away as crowds storm the turnstiles.

It is 1934, England are playing Scotland at Wembley and Frank Moss, the English goalkeeper, is full length on the ground. 'He saved us,' declared the caption writer.

A 1920 crowd at Highbury and something catches the caption writer's eye. 'The increased patronage of women spectators is a marked feature of the new season,' he wrote. Look closely. There are five women in there.

It is 1932, Highbury gets a new stand and the Prince of Wales comes to open it, to see the match – Chelsea v Arsenal – and to meet the teams.

The famous 1953 FA Cup Final at Wembley. A perfect pass from Stanley Matthews, a sure shot from South African Bill Perry and Blackpool win the cup in the last minute.

With the Queen applauding and the stands going wild, Harry Johnston and Stanley Matthews are carried shoulder high after Blackpool's 1953 triumph at Wembley.

March 1958 and the great Johnny Haynes leads Fulham into battle yet again. He joined Fulham straight from school and stayed with the club for his entire career.

June 1913 and Dr W.G.Grace, the most famous cricketer of all time, carefully places a ball in the slips. Dr Grace was a month away from his 65th birthday.

The 1920s and a passion for cricket sweeps the country. In back streets, playgrounds and recs small boys practise.

Left: August 1923 and there's a half-mile queue at The Oval to see Jack Hobbs, the world's leading batsman and a national hero. *Right:* 1931 and Harold Larwood, one of the fastest bowlers of all time, was in devastating action for Nottinghamshire at The Oval. The 'Bodyline' Test series against Australia that made him a legend was just over the horizon.

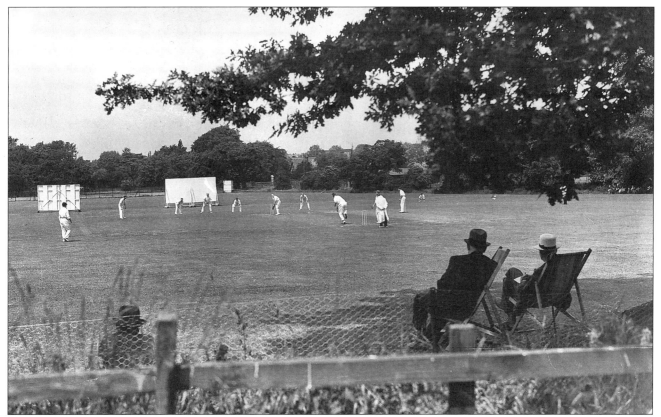

June 1940 and the country is at war but peace briefly breaks out on Dulwich Common. London Counties are playing Honor Oak.

June 1963 and Cassius Clay comes to town. Henry Cooper was our man. He put up a heroic fight but, as his dressing gown declared, Clay was The Greatest.

The early 1920s and Suzanne Lenglen, the sensational French champion, dominates Wimbledon, drawing huge crowds and never losing a match.

Wimbledon, 1934, and Fred Perry is winning the men's singles. He won it the following year, too, and the year after that. The 1930s were golden years for British tennis and everyone loved Fred Perry.

Left: The 1907 Lea Regatta. One of the newly formed ladies' rowing crews in regulation dress: collars, ties, long skirts. *Right:* The 1921 Lea Regatta. Berets, blouses, knickerbockers, black stockings. 'Charming Lea Oarswomen,' read the 1921 caption.

The 1937 Rugby international at Twickenham. Thousands of Welsh supporters roar through London, only to see their team go down 4-3 to England.

29 July 1948: John Mark, 22-year-old medical student, carries the Olympic flame into Wembley Stadium. The XIV Olympiad, London, 1948, can begin.

King George VI, in the uniform of Admiral of the Fleet, watches the March Past of the Nations at the opening of the 1948 Olympic Games at Wembley Stadium.

The 1948 Olympics at Wembley Stadium: 59 nations, 4,500 competitors, the highest number to date.

The world marbles
championships at
Crystal Palace in 1971.
The Penthouse Pets
don't win but get their
pictures in all the
papers.

Kung Fu in Chinatown. A Chinese
athlete brings in the Year of the
Rabbit, otherwise known as 1975.

Fame

To see your name in lights! To stop the traffic! To hear the roar of the crowd! In London it is happening to someone all the time.

1985: a sea of smiles and waving hands. The Live Aid Concert at Wembley.

1912: Budget Day. David Lloyd George, Chancellor of the Exchequer, walks from Downing Street to the House of Commons with his wife.

1924: Dame Nellie Melba making one of her famous farewell appearances at the Albert Hall. She was, as so often, singing Tosti's 'Goodbye'.

1936: Amy Johnson, the charismatic flyer, a superstar of the 1930s, at Croydon aerodrome, about to set a new record for a solo flight from London to Cape Town.

1937: fans mob Hollywood star Robert Taylor, the heart-throb of the year.

1945: VE Day and Mr Churchill gives his famous V sign as his open car slowly edges its way through ecstatic crowds to the House of Commons.

1954: Johnny Ray, appearing
at the Hippodrome, stops the
traffic in Charing Cross Road.

1969: Mick Jagger and the Rolling Stones draw a
multitude to Hyde Park.

1965: The Beatles get an ear-splitting send-off at London Airport when they leave for a two-week coast-to-coast tour of America.

1973: bouquets, garlands and a standing ovation for Maria Callas at the Festival Hall. A huge crowd is waiting at the stage door.

1982: a tumultuous welcome for John Paul II, the first Pope ever to visit Britain.

1985: Bob Geldof singing his heart out at the sensational 16-hour Live Aid concert at a jam-packed Wembley Stadium.

Making a Living

Londoners find a variety of ways to pay the rent.

Cleaning Big Ben. The nation's most famous clock has four faces, each one 22ft in diameter. They all need an occasional wash.

Locking men up.
Before Newgate
Prison came down
in 1902, the
warders were a
familiar sight in
Newgate Street.
That is Chief
Warder Scott
holding the door
open.

Tunnelling. Working on
building the Waterloo and
City Railway in 1894.

Digging. A London building site in 1900.

Conducting buses. Miss Alice Mereday, 18, one of the first London clippies. She was taken on by the London General Omnibus Company in 1917.

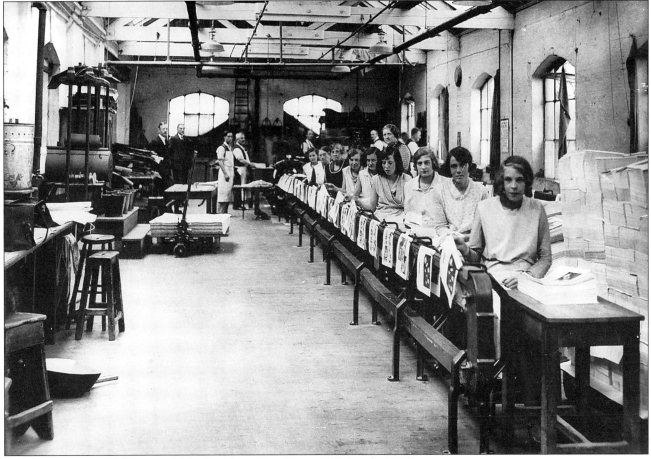

Making books. Stitching and binding for a London publisher in 1931.

Finishing footballs. Seasonal factory work in 1931.

Repairing
shoes.
Customers in
a while-you-
wait shoe
repairer in
Edgware
Road in 1933.

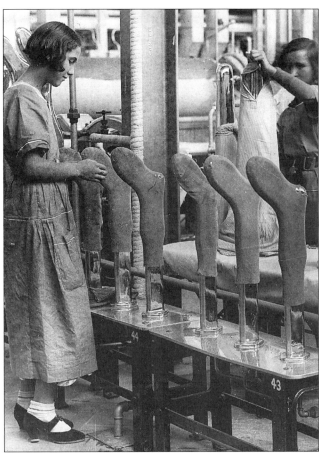

Left: Stitching cricket balls. Norwood was known for it in 1934. *Right:* Drying socks. A sock dryer in the new model laundry at Palmers Green in 1933.

Manning lime kilns. The original lime house of Limehouse, photographed in 1935.

January 1934: thousands of girls today applied for one job at Ray Smith's Library in New Bridge Street.

Making cricket bats. Willow being seasoned in Finchley in 1938.

But just about any job, you might think, is better than no job ...

July 1925: a street corner in Lambeth.

High Society

As Mr Irving Berlin declared:
"Oh I'm Putting on my top hat,
Tying up my white tie,
Brushing up my tails..."
London's the place for that, old bean. Always has been …

Mrs Charles Sweeny in a pageant at Grosvenor House in 1935. She represents Light. Mrs Sweeny later
became the Duchess of Argyll.

June 1919: Lady Diana
Manners, daughter of
the Duke of Rutland,
marries Lieut Duff
Cooper of the
Grenadier Guards at St
Margaret's,
Westminster.

December 1928: the Three Arts Ball at the Piccadilly Hotel.

June 1935: the
Prince of Wales
with Mrs Ernest
Simpson at Royal
Ascot for the
Gold Cup.

June 1935: guests sitting this one out at the Ascot Ball in the Wentworth Club.
The Prince of Wales attended.

June 1935: the Jewels of the Empire Ball at Grosvenor House. Gems worth £2,500,000 are on show, the most spectacular display of jewels London has seen.

June 1935: Queen Charlotte's Birthday Ball at Grosvenor House. The debutantes curtsey while Princess Alice, Countess of Athlone, cuts the 5ft cake.

1 January 1936: seeing in the New Year at the Chelsea Arts Ball in the Royal Albert Hall.

July 1936: debutantes presented to King Edward VIII after heavy rain had ended his first garden reception.

October 1936: the annual Motor Ball at the Royal Opera House.

May 1937: the first big social event of the Coronation season, The Coronation Costume Ball in the Albert Hall.

September 1937:
Penelope Dudley
Ward, star of
French Without
Tears, and actor
Guy Middleton
leave for France on
the Champlain
Boat Train at
Waterloo.

November 1937: the
annual Film Ball at the
Royal Albert Hall.

May 1939: the Royal Caledonian Ball at Grosvenor House.

June 1978: Mr Nubar Gulbenkian collects his new car from Berkeley Square. He has had a standard black London taxi converted into an elegant brougham with wickerwork sides.

On The Town

What will London be doing tonight? Well we are spoiled for choice in these parts. Some, I think you will find, will be doing this. Others will be doing that ...

Soho, 1978.

1874: the Albert Hall, only four years old. To come are years and years of concerts, recitals, charity balls, exhibitions, festivals, boxing matches, proms. What would we do without it?

1907: the original Albert Hall organ, the biggest ever built, 150 tons, nearly 9,000 pipes. Bruckner gave the inaugural concert.

1910. the Alhambra, Leicester Square, the theatre that brought the Diaghilev ballet to London. Its Moorish minarets, huge dome, fountain and grand organ could not save it. The Odeon occupies the site now.

1909: Hamlet at the Lyceum Theatre in Wellington Street. The queue reaches the Strand.

1910: the Empire Theatre in Leicester Square, *en fête* for the Coronation of George V.

Left: 1911: the Gaiety, celebrated musical theatre on the corner of the Strand. It was pulled down in 1957. Citibank is there now. *Right:* 1912 : The Victoria Palace. The statue on top of the dome is Pavlova, the great ballerina, who hated it. It stood there on one toe until the Second World War.

1925: Ben Hur, the silent screen's mighty epic and a smash hit at the Tivoli Cinema in the Strand. Huge queues nightly.

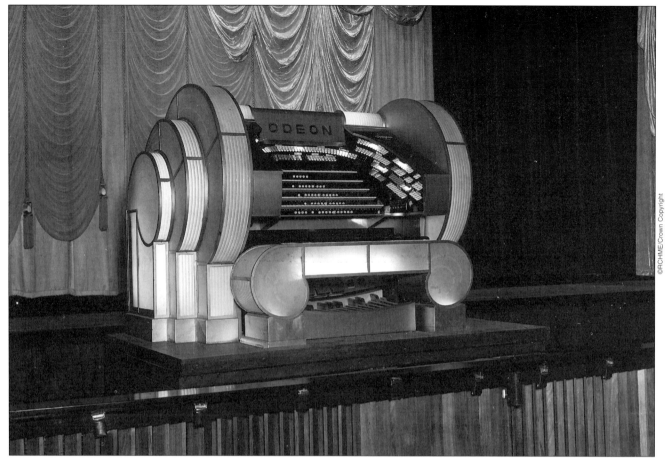

©RCHME/Crown Copyright

1938. the Mighty Wurlitzer having a breather at the Odeon, Leicester Square.

1963: a *pas de deux* at the
Hammersmith Palais.

1964: opening night of The Sporting Club, Knightsbridge.

1964: cabaret at the Pigalle in Piccadilly.

1966: bunny girls at the
Playboy Club.

1966: mass bingo at Wembley.

1965: afternoon bingo in Hackney.

1971: socialising in Paddington.

1977: entertainment in Great Windmill Street …

1978: and in Berwick Street.

1977: a pint or two ...

1961: a bit of a whirl ...

... and a good book in a comfortable chair at your club.

Going Shopping

A crystal ball has revealed what you will do if you win the jackpot in the lottery. You will buy a thing or two. London is certainly the place for that. No city in the world has such shops. You want to know why people come to London from the ends of the earth? They come to go shopping.

1914: afternoon tea table from Aspreys, New Bond Street.

©RCHME/Crown Copyright

Harrods in 1892.

Harrods in 1928.

SEVEN·HOVRS·TO·WORK·TO·SOOTHING·SLVMBER·SEVEN,
TEN·TO·THE·WORLD·ALLOT·AND·ALL·TO·HEAVEN

Liberty Ltd
showroom in
1895.

Morel Cobbett &
Sons, wine
merchants at 210
Piccadilly in 1894.

Fish and game counter at
Slaters, Kensington High
Street, in 1909.

Regent Street in 1921.

Building Department showroom at Barker and Co, Kensington High Street, in 1912.

Electrical Department at Barker and Co, Kensington High Street, in 1912.

Birch, Birch and Co: Wines, liqueurs, iced punch, ices, soups etc.

Ladies Outfitting Department at Harrods in 1919.

Old Bond Street in 1923.

Bargain Day at Curzon Bros in New Bridge Street, 1923. Underwear given away to each purchaser of a suit of clothes. 'At times vehicular traffic was impeded.'

Shoe sale in Barkers in 1928.

Winter sales at the Kensington Drapery Stores in 1929. An early morning queue waits in the rain.

Christmas shopping on Ludgate Hill in 1930.

'On Morning Parade. Girl lift-attendants at the new Gamage store at the Marble Arch being inspected before the public is admitted.' September, 1930.

The summer sale at Harrods in 1934.

Remnant Day at Derry and Toms, Kensington High Street, 1930.

The two-shilling hat counter at Selfridges in 1936.

The winter sale at Harrods in 1937.

Floodlighting at Selfridges in 1937.

Regent Street in 1938.

Designer
boiler suits
and women's
service
uniforms in
West End
windows in
September
1939.

The hat counter at a Salvage Sale Day in Oxford Street after air raids in November 1940. Long before opening time men were forming a huge queue. They were let in a hundred at a time.

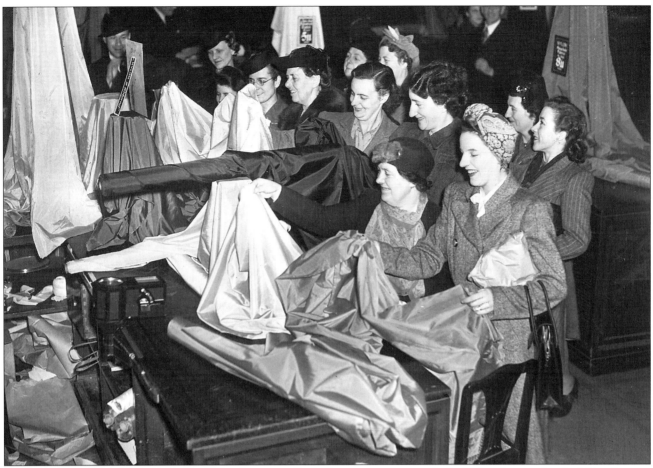

5 November 1945: 'Nylon Arrives. The long-awaited Government parachute Nylon has arrived at Pontings, Kensington. It is two coupons per yard.'

Peter Robinson fashion window in 1956.

The Only Evening Paper

HERE is an image familiar to every Londoner. An orange and white *Evening Standard* van battles through the traffic, part of a fleet of vans whose job is to get the latest edition of the *Evening Standard* to newsagents and street sellers all over Greater London. It is a paper full of local, national and international news, of features, political commentary, cartoons, reviews and advertising, with photographs on virtually every editorial page. It is the very model of a modern metropolitan newspaper. If you live in London you are probably one of its readers.

Who would guess it had been with us for so long? The *Evening Standard* is well into its second century but it has got its second, third and fourth wind and is galloping along. It first appeared in 1827, a new thunderbolt, four pages, price 7d, no punches pulled. Its owner was a young publisher with political ambitions and no time for Mr Canning, the Prime Minister of the day. The editor, Dr Giffard, was said to be irritable, sulky and dangerous. With an unrivalled flight of carrier pigeons and relays of couriers he had the latest news on the street in days.

The *Evening Standard* has changed hands and offices and indeed editors several times since then, also its size, its title and its price. For almost 100 years it was a penny. When they put it up to 1½d in 1951 some people cancelled their subscriptions. It was an evening paper when it started, became a morning paper and then an evening paper again and for 150 years or so it was produced in Shoe Lane just off Fleet Street, most of that time in a solid Victorian building with thundering presses in the basement and a handsome clock over the entrance. Reporters, stubbing out their cigarettes on the lino, hammered out their stories on ancient typewriters. The copy was set in print on hot metal machines still in daily use long after their day had passed.

The evening newspaper field was fiercely competitive. There were nine London evening papers when Edward VII reigned over us but one by one they folded until at last there were only two, the *Evening Standard* and the *Evening News*. In 1980 they merged and London had a single evening paper of singular quality.

It had outlived Shoe Lane. Briefly it moved into the Fleet Street building known as the Black Lubianka taking its clock with it and, in the great newspaper diaspora, made for Kensington where a remarkable building and revolutionary change were waiting. The largest atrium in Europe, wall-climbing glass lifts, mature trees, sophisticated terminals on every desk, an astounding central computer. It was a leap into the millenium.

The *Evening Standard* arrived first, soon to be joined by *The Daily Mail* and *The Mail on Sunday*. Lord Rothermere's three great newspapers are now all housed under one roof and using systems of newspaper technology which lead the world. Outside in Derry Street, high over the entrance to the new Northcliffe House, is a daily reminder of an older technology and of a rumbustious past. The *Evening Standard*, moving into the future, naturally brought its clock.

Paperboys spreading the amazing news: Evening Standard By Aeroplane.

The *Evening Standard* bi-plane, pride of the 1930s.

Late Night Final, Saturday, 21 May 1927. One Hundred Years Old Today.

The Sketch Oct. 21, 192

Vintage Wine

We may envy the man who orders his wines with assurance, but we may be certain that he, too, once envied others. He has spent long years schooling himself to distinguish—not only in wines, but in every sphere of life—between vintage and *vin ordinaire*.

So he has come at last to a knowledge of what is good and what is bad in the art of living, what is true and what is untrue, what is beautiful and what is ugly He has learned to sift the gold of life from the dross.

The "Evening Standard" is edited with a like discretion, and imparts to those who read it a trustworthy judgment of affairs.

Readers of the "Evening Standard," like choosers of good wines, are *gourmets* of life : their palates are trained to perfection.

LET THE

EVENING STANDARD

QUICKEN YOUR SENSE OF VALUES

B12

'Readers of the "Evening Standard", like choosers of good wines, are gourmets of life: their palates are trained to perfection,' declared this *Evening Standard* advertisement in the 1920s. Bang on, of course.

Compositors put the pages together in flat metal formes, each line a separate slug of metal type.

On to the foundry where curved castings of each page are made and clamped on to the waiting rotary presses.

Goodbye to hot metal. Outdated linotype machines leaving the *Evening Standard* in Fleet Street in July 1986.

A linotype machine, a marvel of Victorian ingenuity ... still in use in the 1980s.

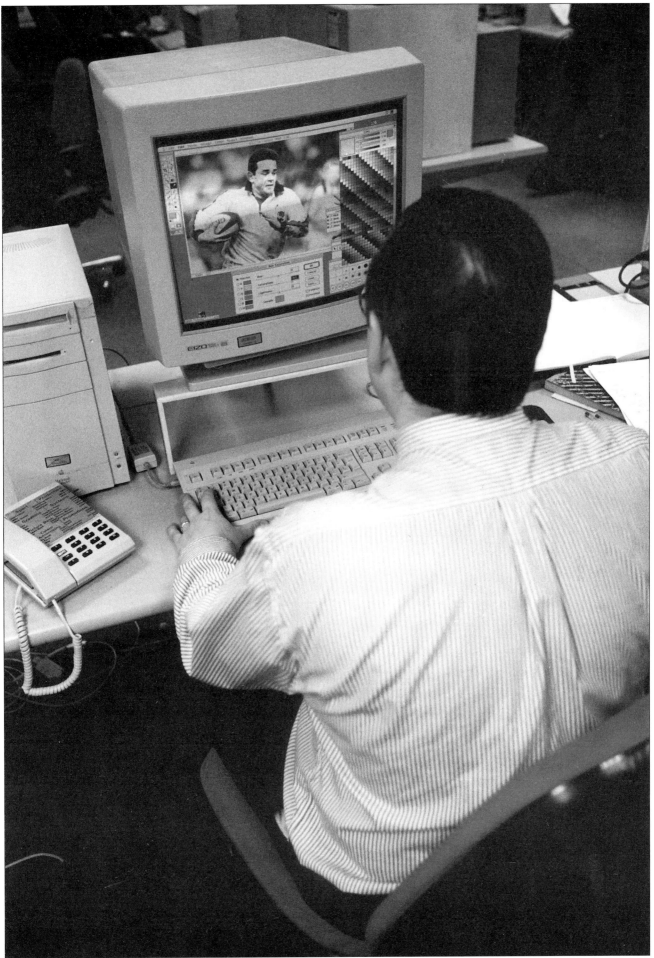

A picture is electronically transmitted from an Apple Macintosh computer in the *Evening Standard* offices in Kensington to presses on the other side of London.

The editorial floor of the 1990s: sub-editors in a new paper-free environment editing, designing and making-up pages on screens linked to a powerful state-of-the-art master computer.

The *Evening Standard* clock. Part of our past, our present and our future.